Silver and Gold

Silver and Gold:

*Your Insurance Policy
Against Monetary Debasement,
the Global Debt Crisis, and Financial
Collapse*

Francis Williams

Silver and Gold: Your Insurance Policy Against Monetary Debasement, the Global Debt Crisis, and Financial Collapse

ISBN: 978-0-9952409-7-1

Published by Quite Frank Educational Services
[Richmond, British Columbia]

This book is a work of research and analysis. While AI tools were used to assist with research, formatting, organization, and editing, the insights, perspectives, and conclusions are the result of human judgment and expertise.

Printed in the USA

.

Cover design by Francis Williams

First Edition: 2025

"Gold is money. Everything else is credit."

~ J.P. Morgan

*"Whoever controls the volume of money
in any country is absolute master of all industry and
commerce."*

~ James A. Garfield, 20th President of the United States

For those who understand and are able…

Be Prepared.

Disclaimer

The information provided in this book is for educational and informational purposes only and should not be construed as financial, investment, tax, legal, or other professional advice. The author and publisher are not financial advisors, investment professionals, or legal experts. Readers are encouraged to conduct their own research and consult with qualified professionals before making any financial or investment decisions. While every effort has been made to ensure the accuracy and reliability of the information contained in this book, the author and publisher make no representations or warranties, express or implied, regarding the completeness, accuracy, or applicability of the content. Economic conditions, market dynamics, and financial regulations are constantly evolving, and past performance is not indicative of future results. Any reliance on the information in this book is strictly at the reader's own risk. Investing in gold, silver, or any other financial assets carries inherent risks, including but not limited to price volatility, market fluctuations, regulatory changes, and geopolitical factors. The value of precious metals and other assets can rise and fall, and there are no guarantees of profit or protection from loss. Furthermore, historical references to financial crises, currency collapses, and monetary policies are included for informational purposes only and should not be interpreted as predictions or guarantees of future events. The author and publisher disclaim any liability for any financial losses, damages, or other consequences that may result from the use of the information in this book. The reader assumes full responsibility for their financial decisions and investment choices.

By reading this book, you acknowledge and agree to the terms of this disclaimer. If you do not agree with these terms, you should not rely on the information provided herein.

Note to the Reader

In the creation of this book, a combination of extensive research, human expertise, and advanced AI tools were utilized to gather, format, organize, and edit the material presented. AI-assisted technology played a role in streamlining the writing process, ensuring clarity, consistency, and coherence in the content while maintaining a high standard of accuracy and readability. However, while AI tools contributed to the structuring and refinement of this book, the core ideas, insights, and analysis are based on historical research, economic principles, and real-world financial trends. The information provided is the result of a careful synthesis of data, expert opinions, and well-documented historical examples, with the ultimate goal of offering readers valuable knowledge and actionable insights. It is important to acknowledge that AI is a tool, not a substitute for human expertise. The perspectives, conclusions, and recommendations in this book reflect thoughtful consideration of economic history and financial strategies, guided by both traditional research methods and modern technological enhancements. As always, I encourage readers to think critically, conduct further research, and seek professional financial advice when making important investment decisions. My hope is that this book provides a strong foundation for understanding the critical role of gold and silver in protecting wealth, especially in uncertain economic times.

Thank you for taking the time to read this book. May it serve as a valuable resource in your journey toward financial security and independence.

Foreword

In an era of economic uncertainty, rising inflation, and mounting global debt, the need for financial security has never been greater. Every generation faces its own economic challenges, but the world today is at a crossroads where reckless monetary policies, excessive government spending, and the erosion of purchasing power have left savers and investors in an increasingly precarious position. While governments assure us that inflation is "transitory" and financial markets remain "resilient," history suggests otherwise.

Throughout history, gold and silver have stood as beacons of stability amid financial turmoil. Empires have risen and fallen, paper currencies have come and gone, but precious metals have remained. They are not merely commodities; they are a form of real money - one that cannot be printed, manipulated, or devalued at the whim of politicians and central bankers. As the global financial system faces unprecedented strain, the case for gold and silver has never been stronger.

I have spent years analyzing global markets, studying economic cycles, and observing the consequences of unsound monetary policies. Time and again, I have seen individuals and institutions place their faith in fiat currencies, only to watch their wealth evaporate as inflation, financial crises, and government interventions take their toll. The lesson is clear: those who fail to understand history are doomed to repeat its mistakes. Those who ignore the enduring value of precious metals may find themselves unprepared when the next financial shock arrives.

This book is not about fear - it is about preparedness. It is about understanding the forces that shape our financial system and taking proactive steps to protect your wealth. Whether you are a seasoned investor or someone just beginning to explore the world of gold and silver, the insights in these pages will equip you with the knowledge to make informed decisions. You will learn not only why monetary debasement is inevitable in a fiat-based system but also how you can use gold and silver as a hedge against it.

In the coming years, we are likely to witness financial upheavals that will reshape the global economy. Governments will continue to inflate away their debt, central banks will push policies that favor short-term stability over long-term soundness, and financial markets will experience extreme volatility. Those who are prepared will not only survive but thrive. Those who remain complacent may find themselves caught in the storm.

The pages ahead offer both a warning and a solution. Gold and silver are not relics of the past; they are the foundation of sound money and the ultimate safeguard against financial collapse. The choice is yours: trust in the promises of politicians and central bankers or take control of your financial future with assets that have stood the test of time.

I encourage you to read this book carefully, absorb its lessons, and take action. The time to prepare is now.

Silver and Gold:

Your Insurance Policy Against Monetary Debasement, the Global Debt Crisis, and Financial Collapse

Table of Contents

Chapter 1: The Track Record for Precious Metals

Why Gold and Silver Have Stood the Test of Time

Throughout history, gold and silver have served as **the most reliable forms of money, wealth preservation, and economic stability**. Unlike **fiat currencies**—which can be printed at will by governments—gold and silver are **finite** resources with intrinsic value. This fundamental difference is why precious metals have endured as the ultimate form of wealth preservation, while countless paper currencies have risen and fallen.

Today, we stand at a **pivotal moment in financial history**. Governments worldwide have accumulated unprecedented levels of debt, central banks have engaged in relentless money printing, and inflation continues to erode the purchasing power of savings. While traditional investments such as stocks, bonds, and savings accounts may appear stable, they are fundamentally tied to fiat currencies that are being actively devalued.

In contrast, gold and silver **cannot be printed**, they **cannot be devalued** by political whims, and they **have survived every economic collapse** in recorded history.

This chapter will explore **why gold and silver remain essential in protecting wealth**, how they have performed in past financial crises, and why they are still **the ultimate insurance policy** against monetary debasement, financial instability, and economic downturns.

The Unique Properties That Make Gold and Silver the Ultimate Stores of Value

Gold and silver have been **used as money for over 5,000 years**, outlasting every paper currency ever created. Their endurance is due to the following key properties:

1. Durability

Unlike paper money, which can **degrade, burn, or become worthless due to hyperinflation**, gold and silver are nearly **indestructible**. A gold coin from ancient Rome still holds value today, whereas most paper currencies issued in the last century are now obsolete.

2. Scarcity and Limited Supply

Governments and central banks can print fiat currency in **unlimited quantities**, but gold and silver **must be mined, refined, and processed**, making them inherently valuable. This **natural scarcity** ensures that gold and silver retain their purchasing power.

3. Divisibility and Portability

Gold and silver can be **divided into smaller units** without losing their intrinsic value. This makes them practical for trade and commerce. Silver, in particular, has historically been used for **day-to-day transactions**, while gold has been the **preferred store of wealth**.

4. Universal Acceptance

Gold and silver are **recognized and valued worldwide**. Unlike fiat currencies, which rely on government trust, gold and silver have intrinsic worth and are accepted **across borders and throughout history**.

5. Intrinsic Value Beyond Money

While fiat money derives value solely from government decree, gold and silver are also used in **technology, medicine, and industry**. Silver, for example, is crucial for **solar panels, electronics, and medical applications**, further increasing its long-term demand.

Gold and Silver vs. Fiat Currency: The Battle of Wealth Preservation

To illustrate why gold and silver have consistently preserved wealth while fiat currencies have failed, let's examine the performance of **historical currencies versus gold and silver**.

Year	Gold Price (USD per oz)	Silver Price (USD per oz)	Purchasing Power of $1 USD (1913 Equivalent)
1913	$20.67	$1.29	$1.00 (100%)
1971	$35.00	$1.50	$0.20 (20%)
2000	$279.11	$5.00	$0.05 (5%)
2024	$2,000+	$25+	**$0.03 (3%)**

The chart above demonstrates the **catastrophic decline in the U.S. dollar's purchasing power** since 1913, while **gold and silver have appreciated in value** over the same period.

Key Takeaway:

- If you held **$100 in cash in 1913**, today it would be worth **about $3 in purchasing power** due to inflation.

- If you held **$100 in gold in 1913**, it would be worth **over $10,000 today** in dollar terms.

- If you held **$100 in silver in 1913**, it would be worth **over $2,000 today** in dollar terms.

This is the essence of why gold and silver matter: **they do not lose value over time, while fiat currencies inevitably do**.

Gold and Silver as a Hedge Against Economic Crises

Gold and silver shine the brightest when **financial turmoil strikes**. Historically, when stock markets collapse, inflation skyrockets, or banking systems fail, people flock to **hard assets**—gold and silver being the most trusted among them.

Here are some **historical examples** of gold and silver acting as a hedge during financial crises:

1. The Great Depression (1929-1939)

During the **stock market crash of 1929**, the U.S. government **confiscated gold from citizens** to prop up the collapsing economy. While paper assets lost nearly **90% of their value**, gold maintained purchasing power, proving its resilience in times of crisis.

2. The 1970s Inflation Crisis

When President Richard Nixon **ended the gold standard in 1971**, the U.S. dollar began **losing value rapidly**. Gold soared from **$35 per ounce in 1971 to over $800 per ounce by 1980**, reflecting the loss of confidence in the fiat system.

3. The 2008 Financial Crisis

The collapse of Lehman Brothers in 2008 sent shockwaves through global markets. Stocks crashed, real estate values plummeted, and **central banks began printing trillions in stimulus money**. Gold responded by surging from **$700 per ounce in 2008 to nearly $1,900 per ounce in 2011**.

4. COVID-19 and 2020-2023 Inflation Surge

During the pandemic, governments **printed unprecedented amounts of money** to stimulate the economy, causing inflation to spike. Gold reached an all-time high, and silver saw massive gains as investors sought **safe-haven assets**.

Key Lesson: Every major economic crisis has resulted in **fiat money losing value and gold/silver increasing in price**.

The Case for Silver: The Overlooked Wealth Preserver

While gold has been the dominant store of value for centuries, **silver offers unique advantages** that make it an equally important investment.

1. Silver is Undervalued Compared to Gold

The **gold-to-silver ratio** (how many ounces of silver it takes to buy one ounce of gold) has historically been around **15:1**. However, in recent years, the ratio has been closer to **80:1 or higher**, meaning silver is **historically cheap relative to gold**.

2. Industrial Demand is Growing

Unlike gold, which is mainly used as a monetary metal, **silver is essential for industrial applications**, including:

- **Solar panels**
- **Electric vehicles (EVs)**
- **Medical technologies**
- **Electronics and batteries**

This ensures **long-term demand** for silver, even beyond investment purposes.

3. Silver is More Affordable for Investors

Gold, at over **$2,000 per ounce**, can be expensive for small investors. Silver, however, at **$25 per ounce**, offers **a more accessible entry point** for wealth preservation.

4. Silver Historically Outperforms Gold in Bull Markets

During past precious metals bull markets, silver has **outperformed gold in percentage terms**. For example:

- In the **1970s**, gold rose **2,300%**, while silver skyrocketed **3,700%**.

- From **2008-2011**, gold doubled, while silver nearly **quadrupled**.

For investors looking for **higher upside potential**, silver presents **a compelling opportunity**.

Conclusion: Gold and Silver as Financial Insurance

In a world of **rising debt, fiat currency devaluation, and economic uncertainty**, **gold and silver stand as the last line of defense against financial chaos**.

They have **outlasted every empire, economic crisis, and monetary collapse**. Whether you are looking to **preserve wealth, hedge against inflation, or protect yourself from financial instability**, investing in **precious metals is not just an option—it's a necessity**.

In the next chapter, we will dive deeper into **why gold and silver remain essential in today's economy and how modern financial policies are setting the stage for their resurgence**.

Chapter 2: The Case for Precious Metals in Today's Economy

Why Gold and Silver Are More Relevant Than Ever

In an era of unprecedented **monetary expansion, debt accumulation, and global financial uncertainty**, the case for owning gold and silver has never been stronger. Governments and central banks are devaluing fiat currencies at an alarming rate, stock markets are propped up by excessive money printing, and inflation is eating away at the purchasing power of savers worldwide.

While the mainstream financial system promotes **stocks, bonds, and fiat savings accounts** as the ideal investment vehicles, history has shown that these assets are **vulnerable to economic downturns, market manipulation, and systemic collapse**. Meanwhile, gold and silver—**real, tangible stores of value**—continue to **outperform and protect wealth** during financial crises.

This chapter will explore **why gold and silver remain critical in today's economy**, the risks posed by fiat currency debasement, and how precious metals offer an essential hedge against modern financial instability.

The Modern Economy: A System Built on Debt and Inflation

To understand why gold and silver are essential, we must first recognize the **flaws in today's financial system**—a system built on:

- **Uncontrolled government spending**
- **Central bank manipulation of money supply**
- **A constant cycle of debt and inflation**
- **The devaluation of fiat currencies**

For decades, world economies have **operated on borrowed time**, relying on **cheap credit and monetary expansion** to sustain growth. However, this artificial prosperity comes at a cost—**a fragile financial system that cannot withstand economic shocks**.

1. Governments Are Printing Money at Unprecedented Rates

Since the 2008 financial crisis, central banks have engaged in **massive money-printing programs** to stimulate the economy. The COVID-19 pandemic accelerated this trend, with governments injecting **trillions of dollars** into the system.

For example:

- **The U.S. Federal Reserve printed more money in 2020 than in the previous 200 years combined.**

- **The European Central Bank and Bank of Japan also expanded their money supply to record levels.**

- **Global debt surpassed $300 trillion in 2023—more than three times the world's total economic output (GDP).**

This massive **currency creation** dilutes the value of money, leading to **higher inflation, weaker purchasing power, and a decline in economic stability**.

2. Inflation: The Silent Destroyer of Wealth

Inflation is often described as the **"hidden tax"** that erodes wealth over time. When central banks print excessive amounts of money, prices rise, and the **real value of wages and savings declines**.

Consider this:

- In **1971**, a loaf of bread in the U.S. cost **$0.25**. Today, it costs **over $3.00**.

- In **1965**, a gallon of gas cost **$0.31**. In 2024, it costs **$4-$6** in many areas.

- In **1913**, $1 could buy what now requires **over $30**.

While governments claim that inflation is "under control," **real-world prices** tell a different story. The reality is that central banks are **actively devaluing fiat currencies**, making everything more expensive over time.

Gold and silver, however, have historically **held their value and even appreciated** during times of inflation.

3. Rising National Debt: A Crisis Waiting to Happen

Governments worldwide have accumulated unsustainable levels of debt. This debt is **financed by printing money and issuing bonds**, creating a system that is **doomed to fail**.

- The **United States national debt** exceeds **$34 trillion** and is growing at a rate of **$1-2 trillion per year**.

- Countries like **Japan, China, and the European Union** are also drowning in debt, with no clear plan to repay it.

- When governments can no longer sustain debt payments, **fiat currencies collapse**—a pattern seen throughout history.

Gold and silver provide **protection against sovereign debt crises**, ensuring that wealth is preserved even if governments default or devalue their currencies.

How Gold and Silver Protect Against Financial Instability

Precious metals act as **financial insurance**, providing stability in a world of economic uncertainty. Below are the key ways that gold and silver protect investors from the flaws of the modern financial system.

1. Gold and Silver Preserve Wealth During Inflation

As **paper money loses purchasing power**, gold and silver have historically **retained and increased in value**.

Historical Examples:

- In **1971**, gold was **$35 per ounce**. By 1980, after a decade of high inflation, it had soared to **$850 per ounce**

- Between **2008 and 2011**, as central banks printed trillions in response to the financial crisis, gold surged from **$700 to nearly $1,900 per ounce**.

- In **2020-2023**, gold hit all-time highs due to inflation concerns and economic instability.

Silver also benefits from inflationary periods, often **outperforming gold in bull markets**.

2. Gold and Silver Are a Hedge Against Market Crashes

Stock markets operate on **confidence**—when that confidence is shaken, markets can collapse overnight.

Examples of Stock Market Crashes:

- **1929** – The Great Depression wiped out **90% of stock market value**.

- **2000-2002** – The Dot-Com Bubble saw tech stocks crash by over **75%**.

- **2008** – The Global Financial Crisis caused the stock market to fall by **over 50%**.

- **2020** – The COVID-19 pandemic triggered the fastest market crash in history.

During these downturns, **gold and silver increased in value**, acting as **safe-haven assets** while stocks plummeted.

3. Precious Metals Offer Protection Against Bank Failures

Banks operate on **fractional reserve banking**, meaning they **only keep a small fraction of depositors' money** in reserves. If too many people withdraw their funds at once, banks **collapse**—as seen in:

- **The Great Depression (1930s):** Thousands of banks failed.

- **The 2008 Financial Crisis:** Major institutions like Lehman Brothers collapsed.

- **The 2023 Banking Crisis:** Regional banks in the U.S. faced liquidity issues, forcing government intervention.

Gold and silver **remove counterparty risk** because **you own them outright**—not as a promise from a financial institution.

Silver's Unique Role: The Overlooked Hedge Against Uncertainty

While gold gets most of the attention, **silver is an equally important asset for investors**. In some ways, it may even be **the better investment**.

1. Silver Is Undervalued Relative to Gold

Historically, the **gold-to-silver ratio** (how many ounces of silver it takes to buy one ounce of gold) has averaged around **15:1**. However, in recent decades, it has hovered around **80:1 or higher**, meaning silver is **historically cheap relative to gold**.

2. Silver Has Growing Industrial Demand

Unlike gold, which is primarily a monetary metal, **silver has major industrial applications**, including:

- **Solar panels**
- **Electric vehicles (EVs)**
- **Medical technology**
- **Electronics and batteries**

As global demand for these industries grows, **silver's price will likely rise** due to supply constraints.

3. Silver Is More Affordable for Small Investors

Gold, at over **$2,000 per ounce**, can be expensive for the average investor. Silver, however, at **$25 per ounce**, allows investors to **buy more metal for less money**.

4. Silver Historically Outperforms Gold in Bull Markets

During past precious metals bull markets:

- In the **1970s**, gold rose **2,300%**, while silver skyrocketed **3,700%**
.
- From **2008-2011**, gold doubled, while silver nearly **quadrupled**.

For investors looking for **higher upside potential**, silver presents **a compelling opportunity**.

Conclusion: Precious Metals Are No Longer Optional—They're Necessary

The modern economy is built on **debt, currency devaluation, and financial manipulation**. The only way to protect wealth is to **own real, tangible assets** that stand outside of government control.

Gold and silver are not just investments—they are **lifelines against economic collapse**.

As we continue this book, we will explore **the historical lessons of money, past financial collapses, and how to take action today** to secure your financial future.

In the next chapter, we'll take a **historical journey into money itself**, examining how governments have repeatedly **debased their currencies—and why precious metals have always survived**.

Chapter 3: A Brief History of Money, Corruption, and Inflation

How Governments Have Destroyed Currencies Throughout History

"Paper money eventually returns to its intrinsic value – zero."

~ Voltaire

Money is one of the most critical inventions of human civilization. It allows people to trade, store wealth, and build economies. But throughout history, **rulers and governments have repeatedly manipulated and debased money to serve their own interests**, often at the expense of the people who rely on it.

From **ancient Rome** to **modern-day fiat currencies**, the pattern remains the same:

1. Governments introduce **sound money** (gold, silver, or asset-backed currency).

2. Over time, **they dilute its value** by adding cheap metals, printing excess money, or abandoning gold/silver backing.

3. This results in **inflation, loss of trust, and financial collapse**.

This chapter will explore how history **proves the case for gold and silver—and why fiat currencies always fail.

The Evolution of Money: From Barter to Precious Metals

Before money existed, people engaged in **barter**, directly exchanging goods and services. But barter had major problems:

- **Lack of common value:** How many chickens equal a cow?

- **No standard unit of trade:** Different regions valued goods differently.

- **Inconvenience:** Carrying physical goods for trade was inefficient.

The Birth of Commodity Money

To solve these problems, societies began using **commodity money**—items that held **intrinsic value** and were widely accepted in trade. Early forms included:

✓ **Shells & beads** (Africa, Native America)

✓ **Salt** (Ancient Rome & China)

✓ **Cattle** (Agrarian societies)

✓ **Silver and gold** (Greece, Rome, China)

Over time, gold and silver became the dominant forms of money because they were:

✓ **Durable** (don't corrode like iron or rot like food)

✓ **Scarce** (cannot be easily counterfeited or created at will)

✓ **Divisible** (can be melted into smaller coins)

✓ **Recognizable** (accepted globally across cultures)

How Governments Have Corrupted Money Throughout History

While gold and silver established **stable economies**, rulers and governments **always sought ways to manipulate money** for their own benefit. Below are key historical examples of **monetary debasement and collapse**.

1. The Roman Empire: The First Major Currency Collapse

The Roman Denarius started as **pure silver** and was used for trade across the empire. But as Rome expanded, emperors needed more money to fund **wars, public projects, and political bribes**. Instead of raising taxes, they **debased the currency** by reducing its silver content.

- **100 AD:** The Denarius was **95% silver**.
- **200 AD:** Reduced to **50% silver** to fund wars.
- **250 AD:** Down to **5% silver**, nearly worthless.

The Result?

- **Hyperinflation**—prices of goods skyrocketed.
- **Loss of public trust**—people rejected Roman coins.
- **Economic collapse**—Rome's financial system crumbled, leading to its decline.

Lesson from Rome: When a government dilutes its money supply, the economy suffers, and collapse follows.

2. The Great Debasement (England, 1544-1551)

King Henry VIII needed **money for wars**, so he **diluted England's silver coins** with cheap metals like copper.

- **Result:** The once-strong English currency **lost value**, and merchants demanded **gold and silver instead of debased coins**.

- **Economic instability followed**, forcing England to restore **higher purity coins** later.

3. The Fall of the Spanish Silver Dollar (16th-17th Century)

Spain became **the richest empire** after discovering **massive silver deposits in South America**. The Spanish **minted silver coins ("Pieces of Eight")**, which became the **global reserve currency** of the time.

But Spain made a **critical mistake**:

    ✗ Instead of **building a productive economy**, they relied solely on **new silver supplies**.

    ✗ The overabundance of silver caused **monetary inflation**, making Spanish goods expensive and uncompetitive.

    ✗ Spain **went bankrupt multiple times** as its empire weakened.

Lesson: Even sound money can lose value if governments flood the market with it without economic productivity.

Paper Money: The Rise and Fall of Fiat Currencies

Gold and silver worked well for centuries, but governments wanted **more control** over money. The solution? **Paper money backed by gold and silver**—at least at first.

4. The First Experiment with Paper Money (China, 11th Century)

China was the **first civilization to introduce paper currency**. It was initially backed by gold and silver, but emperors **printed too much** to finance wars.

- **Result:** Hyperinflation struck, trust in paper money collapsed, and **China returned to silver and gold**.

5. The Weimar Republic (Germany, 1921-1923): The Most Famous Hyperinflation Crisis

After World War I, Germany **owed massive war reparations**. Instead of taxing citizens, the government **printed enormous amounts of paper money** to pay debts.

1918: A loaf of bread cost **0.63 marks**.

1923: The same loaf cost **200 billion marks**

German citizens used **wheelbarrows of money** to buy basic goods.

How Did People Survive?

✓ **Bartering**—people traded goods instead of using worthless paper money.

✓ **Gold & silver**—wealthy individuals **converted their paper money into gold** before hyperinflation set in.

Lesson: Printing money without economic growth leads to hyperinflation and currency collapse.

---

6. The End of the Gold Standard (1971): The U.S. Dollar Becomes Fiat Money

For most of modern history, paper money was **backed by gold**—ensuring that governments couldn't print money **recklessly**.

But in **1971**, President **Richard Nixon ended the gold standard**, meaning the U.S. dollar was no longer **backed by gold**. This allowed the Federal Reserve to **print unlimited dollars**.

Since 1971:

- The U.S. dollar **has lost over 90% of its purchasing power**.

- Prices of goods have skyrocketed.

- **Gold has risen from $35 per ounce to over $2,000 per ounce**.

Lesson: When governments abandon gold-backed money, inflation becomes unavoidable.

What This Means for Today: History is Repeating Itself

Today's financial system is repeating the **same mistakes** as ancient Rome, Weimar Germany, and 1970s America.

✓ **Central banks are printing trillions of dollars.**

✓ **National debts are at record highs.**

✓ **Inflation is eroding purchasing power.**

The only difference? **Now it's on a global scale.**

Gold and silver have **survived every monetary collapse in history—** while every fiat currency has eventually failed.

Conclusion: The Only Safe Money is Gold and Silver

History proves that:

- **Every fiat currency eventually collapses.**

- **Gold and silver have never gone to zero.**

- **Governments will always debase their currency to finance spending.**

As we move into a period of rising debt, inflation, and economic uncertainty, **precious metals are more critical than ever**.

In the next chapter, we will examine the **current global debt crisis and how it threatens the financial system**, making gold and silver even more essential for wealth protection.

Chapter 4: The Global Debt Crisis and the Hidden Tax of Inflation

How Governments Are Destroying Wealth Through Debt and Money Printing

"The problem with fiat money is that governments can print it at will, leading to economic collapse."

~ Ron Paul

Every major economic collapse throughout history has followed a **familiar pattern**:

1. Governments **borrow beyond their means**.

2. When they can't repay the debt, they **print more money** instead of cutting spending.

3. This leads to **inflation**, which silently steals wealth from citizens.

4. Eventually, the debt bubble **bursts**, leading to economic collapse.

Today, **global debt levels are higher than at any point in history**. Central banks and governments insist that debt is "manageable," but the reality is that the financial system is **on the brink of disaster**. In this chapter, we will explore how:

> ✓ **Governments have trapped themselves in an unsustainable debt cycle.**

> ✓ **Inflation is being used as a hidden tax to reduce debt at the public's expense.**

✓ Gold and silver are the only true escape from the coming financial reckoning.

The Scale of the Global Debt Crisis

Unprecedented Debt Levels

As of 2024, the **total global debt exceeds $300 trillion**, more than **three times the world's total economic output (GDP)**. The largest contributors to this crisis are governments, which continuously **borrow money to finance spending they cannot afford**.

- **United States:** Over **$34 trillion** in national debt, growing by **$1-2 trillion per year**.

- **European Union:** Over **$12 trillion** in combined government debt.

- **Japan:** Debt exceeds **260% of its GDP**, the highest in the world.

- **China:** While exact figures are unclear, total debt is estimated at over **$50 trillion**.

The world is drowning in debt. And rather than solving the problem, governments are making it worse.

How Did We Get Here? The Root Causes of the Debt Crisis

1. The End of the Gold Standard

Before 1971, the U.S. dollar was **backed by gold**, meaning the government couldn't print money without sufficient gold reserves. This limited government spending and prevented excessive borrowing.

But when President **Richard Nixon ended the gold standard**, the Federal Reserve gained the ability to **print unlimited dollars**. This led to **massive government debt expansion**—since there were **no longer any constraints**.

2. Central Banks' Addiction to Cheap Money

To stimulate economic growth, central banks **artificially lowered interest rates** for decades. This made borrowing cheap, encouraging **governments, corporations, and individuals to take on excessive debt**.

- After the **2008 financial crisis**, interest rates were cut to nearly **zero** to "boost the economy."

- In response to **COVID-19**, central banks printed **trillions** in stimulus, further inflating debt levels.

Now, as interest rates **rise**, governments and businesses **can't afford their debt payments**, leading to a **ticking time bomb**.

3. Deficit Spending: Governments Spending More Than They Earn

Most governments operate at a **deficit**, meaning they spend more than they collect in taxes. To make up the difference, they **borrow money by issuing government bonds**.

But instead of **paying down debt**, they **keep borrowing more**, making the problem worse.

Example:

- In **2023**, the U.S. government **collected** $4.9 trillion in revenue but **spent** $6.1 trillion, adding **$1.2 trillion** to the national debt in a single year.

- Japan's government debt is **so large** that it cannot be repaid without massive inflation or default.

This endless **borrowing and spending cycle** is **unsustainable—**eventually, something has to break.

Inflation: The Hidden Tax That Steals Your Wealth

When governments accumulate **too much debt**, they have three choices:

1. **Raise taxes** (unpopular and politically risky).

2. **Default on the debt** (destroys trust in the currency).

3. **Print more money to inflate away the debt.**

Governments almost **always** choose Option #3—because it allows them to **silently tax the population** without people realizing it. This is why inflation is called the **"hidden tax."**

How Inflation Works Against You

When governments **print more money**, the value of each existing dollar decreases. This means:

✓ The price of **food, housing, and energy rises.**
✓ The real value of **your savings declines.**
✓ Wages fail to **keep up with rising costs.**

Example:

- **1970s:** A gallon of gas cost **$0.36**.

- **Today:** The same gallon costs **$4.00+** in many areas.

- **That's over 1,000% inflation**—but your wages haven't increased by that much, have they?

The more money the government prints, the **poorer the average citizen becomes**.

Meanwhile, those who own gold and silver are protected—because metals retain their value, while paper money loses purchasing power.

Lessons from History: The Consequences of Debt and Inflation

Throughout history, every government that **tried to print its way out of debt** has failed. Here are some of the worst cases of monetary collapse due to excessive debt and inflation.

1. Weimar Germany (1921-1923)

- The German government printed massive amounts of paper money to pay war debts.

- **Hyperinflation skyrocketed**, and prices **doubled every few days**.

- A loaf of bread went from **0.63 marks in 1918 to 200 billion marks by 1923**.

- **People used wheelbarrows of money** just to buy basic goods.

2. Zimbabwe (2000s)

- The Zimbabwean government **printed money endlessly**, leading to **inflation of 79.6 billion percent per month**.

- **Paper money became worthless**, and people turned to **gold, silver, and foreign currencies** for survival.

3. Venezuela (2010s-Present)

- The government printed excessive money to fund social programs.

- Inflation exceeded **1,000,000%**, making the national currency useless.

- Citizens began **melting down jewelry and trading gold and silver for food and medicine.**

Key Lesson: When a country prints too much money, it destroys its economy. Only **gold and silver retain value during currency collapses.**

Gold and Silver: The Only Protection Against the Debt Crisis

With government debt spiraling out of control, gold and silver **offer a way to escape the destruction of fiat currency**.

1. Precious Metals Hold Their Value

While paper money loses purchasing power, gold and silver have **maintained their value for thousands of years**.

- In **1913**, $1 could buy **20 loaves of bread**.

- Today, **$1 buys less than a single loaf**.

- But **an ounce of gold** in 1913 could buy **a high-quality suit—** and today, it still can.

2. Central Banks Themselves Are Buying Gold

Governments and central banks **know their fiat currencies are weak**. That's why, despite discouraging the public from buying gold, **they are stockpiling it themselves**.

- In **2022**, central banks bought more gold than in any year since 1967.

- China, Russia, and India are **hoarding gold to reduce reliance on the U.S. dollar.**

3. Gold and Silver Are Crisis-Proof

If inflation spirals out of control or a **currency collapse occurs**, **gold and silver will always be valuable**.

✓ **Gold is a long-term store of value.**

✓ **Silver is affordable and widely used in industry.**

✓ **Unlike fiat money, gold and silver cannot be printed into oblivion.**

Conclusion: Prepare for the Debt Reckoning

The global debt crisis is **unsustainable**, and governments are using **inflation to steal wealth from the public**. History shows that when a currency collapses, gold and silver **become the only reliable money**.

As we move forward, the next chapter will **explore how monetary debasement erodes wealth—and why precious metals are the only true defense against economic manipulation.**

Chapter 5: The Hidden Tax of Monetary Debasement – How Governments Erode Your Wealth

"Inflation is taxation without legislation."

~ Milton Friedman

Most people think of taxes as money explicitly taken by the government in the form of **income tax, sales tax, or property tax**. However, there is another, **more insidious tax**—one that affects every person who uses fiat currency. This is **monetary debasement**, the gradual destruction of a currency's purchasing power through **inflation, money printing, and reckless government policies**.

Unlike direct taxation, monetary debasement is **invisible to most people**. It does not appear as a deduction on your paycheck or an annual bill from the government. Instead, it **slowly erodes the value of your savings**, weakens wages, and increases the cost of living. Over time, it **transfers wealth from the people to the government and the financial elite**, enriching those who control the money supply while **impoverishing those who rely on it**.

This chapter will explore:

✓ **How monetary debasement works** and why it is the ultimate hidden tax.

✓ **How inflation quietly robs you of your purchasing power.**

✓ **Historical examples of monetary debasement and its consequences.**

✓ **Why gold and silver are the best defense against currency manipulation.**

Understanding Monetary Debasement

Monetary debasement occurs when a government or central bank **reduces the real value of its currency**. This can happen in two ways:

1. **Increasing the money supply (printing more currency)** without an increase in real economic productivity.

2. **Reducing the actual metal content of coins** (as seen in history with silver and gold-based money).

The result? **Each unit of currency buys fewer goods and services over time**.

For the average citizen, this means

✓ The cost of food, housing, healthcare, and education **keeps rising**
.

✓ Wages **fail to keep up** with inflation, making it harder to maintain a good standard of living.

✓ **Savings in the bank lose value** over time.

Governments and central banks present inflation as **a normal economic event**, but in reality, it is **a form of wealth confiscation**.

A Historical Perspective on Monetary Debasement

The concept of monetary debasement is not new—it has been used by rulers and governments **for centuries** to fund wars, expand political power, and bail out failing economies. Let's look at some historical examples.

1. Ancient Rome: The Debasement of the Denarius

The **Roman Empire's silver denarius** was one of the most trusted currencies of its time. However, as Rome expanded and needed more money to finance its empire, emperors **gradually reduced the silver content** in coins.

- **100 AD:** The denarius was **95% silver**.

- **200 AD:** Reduced to **50% silver** to fund wars.

- **250 AD:** Down to **5% silver**, making the currency nearly worthless.

The Result?

- Hyperinflation—prices of goods **skyrocketed**.

- Loss of trust—people **abandoned Roman coins** and returned to bartering.

- Economic collapse—the Roman economy **fell into ruin**, contributing to the empire's decline.

Lesson: When governments dilute their currency's value, economic stability collapses.

2. The Weimar Republic (Germany, 1921-1923) – Hyperinflation at Its Worst

After World War I, Germany had massive war debts and chose to **print enormous amounts of money** instead of raising taxes or cutting spending.

1918: A loaf of bread cost **0.63 marks**.

1923: The same loaf cost **200 billion marks**.

German citizens **carried wheelbarrows of money** just to buy basic goods.

How Did People Survive?

✓ Bartering—people traded goods instead of using worthless paper money.

✓ Gold & silver—wealthy individuals **converted their paper money into gold** before hyperinflation took hold.

Lesson: When governments print excessive money, currency collapses. Precious metals **hold their value** while fiat money becomes worthless.

3. The United States (1971-Present) – The End of the Gold Standard

For most of U.S. history, the dollar was **backed by gold**, meaning every paper dollar could be exchanged for **physical gold**. This **prevented excessive money printing**.

However, in **1971**, President Richard Nixon **ended the gold standard**, allowing the Federal Reserve to **print unlimited dollars**. Since then:

- The **U.S. dollar has lost over 90% of its purchasing power**.

- The price of gold has **risen from $35 per ounce in 1971 to over $2,000 per ounce today**.

- Prices of goods have **skyrocketed**, while wages have failed to keep up.

Lesson: When a government abandons sound money, inflation becomes inevitable, and people's purchasing power declines.

How Monetary Debasement Affects You

Monetary debasement impacts everyone, but it **hurts the middle class and working people the most**. Here's how:

1. Rising Cost of Living

As a currency loses value, the price of goods **increases**. Over time, inflation **reduces how much a paycheck can buy**.

Item	Price in 1970	Price Today (2024)
Gallon of Gas	$0.36	$4.00 - $6.00
New House	$23,000	$400,000+
College Tuition	$500/year	$30,000+/year

Wages have not kept up with these price increases, meaning most people are **poorer than they were decades ago**.

---

2. Erosion of Savings

If you save money in a bank account that pays **less interest than inflation**, you are **losing purchasing power** every year.

Example:

- In the 1980s, savings accounts **paid 5-7% interest**, keeping up with inflation.

- Today, banks **pay less than 1%**, while inflation is **5% or higher**.

- This means that every year, **your money in the bank is worth less in real terms**.

Key Takeaway: Saving in fiat currency is a guaranteed way to lose wealth over time.

Gold and Silver: The Ultimate Protection Against Monetary Debasement

Throughout history, gold and silver have **acted as a hedge** against monetary debasement. Here's why:

1. Gold and Silver Cannot Be Printed

Unlike fiat money, gold and silver **cannot be created out of thin air**. This makes them resistant to **government manipulation and inflation**.

2. Precious Metals Preserve Purchasing Power

Gold and silver have historically **maintained their value over time**. Consider this:

- In **1900**, a $20 gold coin could buy a high-quality **tailored suit**.

- In **2024**, that same gold coin (now worth over **$2,000**) **still buys a high-quality suit**.

- Meanwhile, **$20 in paper money from 1900 is almost worthless today**.

Gold and silver hold their value—fiat money does not.

3. Central Banks Themselves Are Buying Gold

Even though governments push the **"fiat money system,"** central banks are quietly **stockpiling gold**.

- In **2022**, central banks purchased more gold than any year since 1967.

- China, Russia, and India are **hoarding gold to reduce reliance on the U.S. dollar**.

- If gold were obsolete, **why are the world's biggest financial institutions buying it?**

Conclusion: Protect Yourself Before It's Too Late

Monetary debasement is **the silent destroyer of wealth**. Governments and central banks will **continue printing money**, causing inflation to **erode savings and wages**.

Gold and silver **are the antidote** to this financial deception. They are not just investments—they are **real money** that has withstood every economic collapse in history.

As we move forward, the next chapter will explore **how central banks actively work against sound money—and how their policies shape the global financial system to their advantage.**

Chapter 6: Central Banks and Their War on Sound Money

How Governments and Financial Institutions Undermine Gold and Silver to Maintain Control

"Give me control of a nation's money supply, and I care not who makes its laws."

~ Mayer Amschel Rothschild, Banker

Central banks **control the global financial system**. They set interest rates, print money, and influence economies worldwide. While they claim to promote **stability**, their policies often create **inflation, asset bubbles, and financial crises**.

The biggest threat to central banks? **Gold and silver.**

Unlike fiat currencies, gold and silver **cannot be printed or manipulated**. They impose **financial discipline**, preventing governments from **borrowing recklessly and inflating the money supply**. This is why central banks have **waged a long-standing war against sound money**—they need to control the economy, and that means discouraging people from **owning real assets like gold and silver**.

This chapter will uncover:

✓ **Why central banks fear gold and silver.**

✓ **How they manipulate financial systems to keep fiat currency dominant.**

✓ **Why their policies make gold and silver even more essential today.**

What Are Central Banks and How Do They Operate?

A **central bank** is a financial institution that **controls a country's money supply**, sets interest rates, and oversees banking operations. Some of the world's most powerful central banks include:

✓ **The Federal Reserve (U.S.)**

✓ **The European Central Bank (ECB)**

✓ **The Bank of England (BoE)**

✓ **The Bank of Japan (BoJ)**

✓ **The People's Bank of China (PBoC)**

Unlike commercial banks that serve individuals and businesses, **central banks serve governments and financial institutions**. Their **policies affect everything** from inflation and employment to stock markets and real estate.

Core Functions of Central Banks:

1. **Issuing Fiat Currency** – Central banks create **paper money** without real backing.

2. **Setting Interest Rates** – By adjusting rates, they influence **borrowing, lending, and economic growth**.

3. **Managing Inflation** – They claim to keep inflation stable, but their policies often **cause inflation instead**.

4. **Regulating Banks** – They oversee commercial banks and act as a **lender of last resort during financial crises**.

While central banks **claim to promote financial stability**, history shows that their **policies create instability instead**.

The War on Sound Money: Why Central Banks Oppose Gold and Silver

For most of human history, economies operated under **gold and silver-backed money**. This prevented governments from **recklessly printing money and accumulating debt**. But over the past century, central banks have done **everything possible to remove gold and silver from the financial system**.

1. The Abandonment of the Gold Standard

For centuries, the world operated under a **gold standard**, meaning that **paper money was backed by a fixed amount of gold**. This system **prevented governments from inflating the money supply**, ensuring financial discipline.

However, central banks and governments found the **gold standard too restrictive**. They wanted to **borrow and print money without limits**, so they systematically **dismantled the gold standard**.

- **In 1933, U.S. President Franklin D. Roosevelt confiscated gold** from American citizens, making private gold ownership illegal.

- **In 1971, U.S. President Richard Nixon officially ended the gold standard**, allowing the Federal Reserve to print **unlimited dollars**.

Once the gold standard was eliminated, central banks could **inflate the money supply at will**, leading to decades of **currency devaluation and rising debt**.

2. Manipulating Interest Rates to Control the Economy

Central banks manipulate **interest rates** to **artificially control economic growth and recessions**.

> ✓ **Low interest rates encourage borrowing and speculation**, leading to asset bubbles in **stocks, real estate, and bonds**.

> ✓ **High interest rates slow down the economy**, causing recessions and financial crises.

This **cycle of boom and bust** is **not natural**—it is created by central banks **manipulating the economy**.

If money were still backed by gold and silver, this type of manipulation would be impossible.

3. Printing Money and Causing Inflation

With **no gold standard to limit them**, central banks have **printed trillions of dollars, euros, yen, and other fiat currencies**, devaluing money worldwide.

Example:

- In **2008**, after the financial crisis, central banks **printed trillions of dollars** to bail out banks.

- In **2020-2023**, governments **printed even more money** during the COVID-19 pandemic, leading to **record inflation**.

Instead of solving economic problems, **money printing creates new problems—higher living costs, weaker savings, and extreme market volatility**.

4. Suppressing Gold and Silver Prices

If gold and silver were widely used as money, it would **expose the weakness of fiat currencies**. This is why central banks **actively suppress gold and silver prices** through:

> ✓ **Paper gold markets (ETFs, futures contracts)** – Banks sell **"paper gold"** that isn't backed by real metal, artificially increasing supply
> .
> ✓ **Gold leasing and central bank sales** – Central banks **lease or sell gold** to manipulate prices.
>
> ✓ **Media propaganda** – Financial institutions **downplay gold and silver** while promoting fiat investments.

Despite these efforts, gold and silver have **continued to rise in value over the long term**, proving their resilience against central bank manipulation.

The Consequences of Central Bank Policies

Central banks claim to promote **financial stability**, but their actions have led to **economic disasters**. Here are the biggest consequences:

1. Currency Devaluation and Loss of Purchasing Power

Since the **Federal Reserve was created in 1913**, the **U.S. dollar has lost over 90% of its value**. Other fiat currencies have suffered **similar declines**.

- **In Venezuela, Argentina, and Turkey**, hyperinflation has destroyed savings, forcing citizens to **turn to gold, silver, and cryptocurrencies**.

- **In Japan, decades of low interest rates and excessive debt** have caused economic stagnation.

As central banks **continue printing money**, fiat currencies will **keep losing value**, making gold and silver even more important for **wealth preservation**.

2. Rising Debt and Financial Crises

Central banks **enable governments to borrow recklessly** by keeping interest rates low. This has created a **global debt bubble** that threatens to collapse.

> ✓ **The U.S. national debt exceeds $34 trillion**, with no realistic way to repay it.

> ✓ **Global debt surpasses $300 trillion**, increasing the risk of a financial meltdown.

When the debt bubble bursts, **fiat currencies will decline rapidly, making gold and silver essential for protecting wealth**.

3. Wealth Inequality and Asset Bubbles

Central bank policies **benefit the wealthy** while hurting ordinary people.

> ✓ **Stock and real estate prices rise due to cheap money**, benefiting investors.

> ✓ **Wages stagnate, while living costs soar**, hurting workers.

> ✓ **Middle-class wealth declines**, as savings lose value.

Gold and silver offer ordinary people a way to escape the central banking trap and protect their financial future.

Gold and Silver: The Solution to Central Bank Manipulation

Despite central banks' efforts to suppress them, **gold and silver remain the best hedge against financial instability**.

> ✓ **They cannot be printed or manipulated like fiat currency.**

> ✓ **They preserve purchasing power over decades and centuries.**

> ✓ **They offer financial independence, outside the control of central banks and governments.**

Even Central Banks Are Buying Gold

Despite publicly discouraging gold ownership, central banks themselves are **hoarding gold at record levels**.

> ✓ Russia and China are stockpiling gold to reduce reliance on the **U.S. dollar**.

> ✓ Central banks worldwide **are buying gold at the fastest pace in 50 years**.

If central banks themselves are buying gold, **shouldn't individuals do the same?**

Conclusion: Prepare for the Central Bank Endgame

Central banks have spent decades trying to **eliminate sound money**, replacing it with fiat currency **they can manipulate at will**. But history shows that **every fiat currency eventually fails**, while **gold and silver stand the test of time**.

As the **global financial system faces increasing risks**—rising debt, inflation, and economic instability—**gold and silver offer the best protection against central bank recklessness**.

In the next chapter, we will explore **historical cases of hyperinflation and currency collapses**, showing why nations and individuals who ignore the importance of sound money **always pay the price**.

Chapter 7: Lessons from Hyperinflation and Currency Collapses

Why Fiat Money Always Fails and How Gold and Silver Have Saved Wealth Throughout History

For thousands of years, civilizations have experimented with different forms of money. But every time governments have **replaced gold and silver with fiat currency**, the result has been the same: **inflation, hyperinflation, and economic collapse**.

Today, most people assume their **modern currencies—dollars, euros, yen—will always hold value**. But history tells us otherwise. Every fiat currency in history has eventually **failed**, while gold and silver have always remained valuable.

This chapter explores some of the worst **hyperinflation events and currency collapses** in history, showing how people who relied on fiat money lost everything—while those who held **gold and silver preserved their wealth**.

What is Hyperinflation?

Hyperinflation occurs when a **government prints excessive money**, causing prices to **skyrocket uncontrollably**. This destroys the value of a currency, making it **worthless** in a short period.

Economists define hyperinflation as **monthly inflation exceeding 50%** - meaning prices **double every few weeks**. But in extreme cases, prices can rise **daily or even hourly**, making life impossible for citizens.

When hyperinflation strikes:

✓ **Savings are wiped out**—Bank accounts become worthless.

✓ **Wages become meaningless**—A paycheck won't even buy a loaf of bread.

✓ **People abandon their currency**—They switch to gold, silver, or foreign money.

Every fiat currency in history has faced **some level of inflation**—but some have completely collapsed, leaving people with **nothing**.

Famous Hyperinflation Events and Currency Collapses

1. Weimar Germany (1921-1923): Wheelbarrows of Money

After **World War I**, Germany was burdened with **massive war debt**. Instead of taxing citizens or cutting spending, the government **printed money** to pay reparations.

What happened next?

✓ In **1918**, a loaf of bread cost **0.63 marks**.

✓ By **1922**, it cost **160 marks**.

✓ By **late 1923**, the same loaf cost **200 billion marks**.

People used **wheelbarrows of cash** just to buy groceries. Money was so worthless that::

> ✓ Workers demanded to be paid **twice a day** before their wages lost value
> .
> ✓ People **burned money for fuel** because it was cheaper than firewood.
>
> ✓ **Gold and silver holders thrived**—one ounce of gold could buy an entire city block.

Lesson: When a currency collapses, people are forced to abandon it. Those who own gold and silver survive.

2. Zimbabwe (2000s): 100 Trillion Dollar Bills

Zimbabwe was once a wealthy African nation, but **excessive money printing and government corruption** led to one of the worst hyperinflation cases in history.

- In **1980**, $1 Zimbabwean dollar was equal to **$1.50 USD**.

- By **2008**, Zimbabwe was printing **100 trillion dollar banknotes**—which couldn't buy a loaf of bread
  .
- Inflation hit **89.7 sextillion percent (that's 89,700,000,000,000,000,000,000%)**.

To survive, citizens abandoned their own currency and switched to:

> ✓ **Gold and silver jewelry for trade.**
> ✓ **Foreign currencies like U.S. dollars.**
> ✓ **Bitcoin and other digital assets in later years.**

Lesson: When a government destroys its currency, the people turn to **gold, silver, and alternative money** to survive.

3. Venezuela (2010s-Present): The Collapse of a Nation

Venezuela was once the richest country in South America, with the **largest oil reserves in the world**. But government mismanagement, excessive spending, and money printing led to **hyperinflation and economic ruin**.

Between **2010 and 2020**:

> ✓ Inflation exceeded **1,000,000%**.
> ✓ The Venezuelan **bolivar became worthless**.
> ✓ **Gold and silver became essential**—people melted jewelry to buy food.

Those who **stored wealth in precious metals** survived. Those who **held paper money lost everything**.

Lesson: Even resource-rich countries can collapse if they abandon **sound money** and print fiat recklessly.

4. Argentina (1970s-Present): A Nation Trapped in Inflation

Argentina has suffered repeated **currency collapses** due to money printing and government corruption.

- In the **1980s**, Argentina experienced **hyperinflation** exceeding **5,000% per year**.

- The government kept **replacing its currency**—from the peso to the austral and back again.

- In **2023**, inflation hit **over 100%**, making the Argentine peso nearly worthless.

How did people protect themselves?

✓ **Buying gold and silver**—Argentinians who held metals retained wealth.

✓ **Using U.S. dollars and foreign currencies**.

✓ **Investing in real assets (land, food, and hard commodities).**

Lesson: When fiat money fails, people seek **hard assets that hold value—gold and silver are always first choices**.

The Patterns of Hyperinflation: What Can We Learn?

Every hyperinflation event follows a **clear pattern**:

1. **The government prints too much money.**

2. **The currency loses value, and prices rise rapidly.**

3. **People panic and seek alternative money (gold, silver, foreign currencies).**

4. **The local currency collapses, and the economy is ruined.**

Governments always **blame businesses, foreign countries, or market forces**—but the real cause is **their own reckless money printing**.

Gold and silver have NEVER failed. Every time a currency collapses, **precious metals retain purchasing power**.

Why Gold and Silver Are the Ultimate Protection Against Currency Collapse

✓ **Cannot be printed** – Unlike paper money, gold and silver **cannot be artificially created**.

✓ **Globally recognized** – No matter where you are, precious metals have value.

✓ **Holds purchasing power** – 100 years ago, 1 ounce of gold could buy a **high-quality suit**. Today, it still can.

✓ **Portable wealth** – In every currency crisis, those who **escaped with gold and silver retained their financial freedom**.

Even Governments Are Buying Gold

- China, Russia, and India are **stockpiling gold to reduce reliance on the U.S. dollar**.

- Central banks bought **the most gold in 50 years** in 2022.

- Why? Because **fiat money is losing value worldwide**.

If governments are buying gold, shouldn't you?

Conclusion: Protect Yourself Before the Next Currency Crisis

History shows that fiat money **always fails**. Whether in ancient Rome, Weimar Germany, Zimbabwe, or Venezuela, **currencies collapse when governments print too much money**.

> ✓ **Gold and silver have outlasted every currency collapse in history.**

> ✓ **Governments and central banks cannot print more gold and silver.**

> ✓ **When fiat money fails, precious metals are the last line of financial defense.**

In the next chapter, we will explore **the modern case for investing in gold and silver—why NOW is the best time to buy and how to start building your precious metals portfolio.**

Chapter 8: Investing in Gold and Silver – A Practical Guide

Why Now is the Best Time to Buy and How to Start Building Your Precious Metals Portfolio

"If you don't own gold, you know neither history nor economics."

~ Ray Dalio, Billionaire Investor

Throughout history, gold and silver have protected wealth **during economic crises, inflation, and currency collapses**. Today, as governments print money at record levels and global debt continues to rise, the need to **own real, tangible assets** has never been greater.

This chapter will provide a **step-by-step guide on how to invest in gold and silver**, covering:

✓ **The different ways to invest in gold and silver.**

✓ **Physical metals vs. paper gold/silver: What's best?**

✓ **How to buy gold and silver without getting scammed.**

✓ **How to store and protect your investment.**

Why Now is the Best Time to Invest in Gold and Silver

If history has taught us anything, it's that **fiat currencies always lose value over time**, while gold and silver **maintain purchasing power**. But today, we're facing an even greater crisis.

1. Governments Are Printing Money Like Never Before

Since the **2008 financial crisis**, central banks have printed **trillions of dollars, euros, and yen** to prop up the global economy. The COVID-19 pandemic **accelerated money printing**, leading to:

✓ Record inflation.

✓ Rising debt levels worldwide.

✓ Loss of purchasing power for fiat currencies.

As governments **continue devaluing money**, gold and silver will only become **more valuable**.

---

2. Gold and Silver Are Undervalued Compared to Stocks and Real Estate

✓ Stock markets are at **all-time highs**, inflated by cheap money.

✓ Real estate prices have skyrocketed, making it harder to invest.

✓ Gold and silver, despite recent gains, are still **cheap relative to historical trends**.

Historically, when inflation **rises above 5%**, gold and silver see **major price surges**. With inflation soaring, **now is the time to invest.**

How to Invest in Gold and Silver: The Best Options

There are several ways to invest in precious metals, each with its own advantages and risks.

---

1. Physical Gold and Silver (Best for Long-Term Wealth Preservation)

Owning **physical gold and silver** means you have **direct control over your wealth**. Unlike digital assets or stocks, **you don't rely on a third party**—you own the real thing.

Types of Physical Gold and Silver:

✓ **Coins** – Popular for small investors. Examples:

- **Gold Coins**: American Gold Eagle, Canadian Maple Leaf, South African Krugerrand.

- **Silver Coins**: American Silver Eagle, Canadian Silver Maple Leaf, Austrian Philharmonic.

✓ **Bars** – Best for large investments. Examples:

- **Gold Bars**: 1 oz, 10 oz, 1 kg, or 400 oz bars.

- **Silver Bars**: 1 oz, 10 oz, 100 oz, or 1,000 oz bars.

✓ **Junk Silver** – Old U.S. coins (pre-1965 dimes, quarters, half dollars) contain **90% silver** and can be a **cheap way to accumulate silver**.

Pros of Physical Metals:

✓ No counterparty risk—you own it outright.

✓ Cannot be hacked, seized, or frozen like bank accounts.

✓ Protects against inflation and financial collapse.

Cons of Physical Metals:

✗ Requires safe storage.

✗ Can have higher premiums over spot price.

Best For: Long-term wealth preservation, inflation protection, financial security.

---

2. Gold and Silver ETFs (Paper Metals – Easy but Risky)

Exchange-Traded Funds (ETFs) allow investors to **buy gold and silver on stock exchanges** without holding physical metal.

✓ **Popular Gold ETFs**: SPDR Gold Shares (GLD), iShares Gold Trust (IAU)

✓ **Popular Silver ETFs**: iShares Silver Trust (SLV).

Pros of ETFs:

✓ Easy to buy and sell like stocks.

✓ No need for storage or security.

✓ Good for short-term trading.

Cons of ETFs:

✗ You don't actually own the metal—only a paper claim.

✗ Some funds don't have full metal backing (risk of default).

✗ Could be frozen or restricted in a crisis.

Best For: Short-term trading, portfolio diversification.

3. Gold and Silver Mining Stocks (High Risk, High Reward)

Mining stocks allow you to invest in **companies that produce gold and silver**. If metal prices rise, mining stocks can **increase even more** due to profit growth.

✓ **Gold Miners:** Barrick Gold (GOLD), Newmont Corporation (NEM), Agnico Eagle Mines (AEM).

✓ **Silver Miners:** First Majestic Silver (AG), Pan American Silver (PAAS), Hecla Mining (HL).

Pros of Mining Stocks:

✓ Potential for higher returns than physical metals.

✓ Some pay dividends.

Cons of Mining Stocks:

✗ More volatile than gold and silver.

✗ Companies can fail, go bankrupt, or mismanage resources.

Best For: High-risk investors looking for big gains.

Where to Buy Gold and Silver (Without Getting Scammed)

With rising demand for precious metals, **scammers and fake dealers are everywhere**. Be cautious and only buy from **trusted sources**.

Reputable Online Dealers:

✓ **APMEX** – One of the largest and most trusted bullion dealers.

✓ **JM Bullion** – Good pricing and selection of gold and silver products.

✓ **SD Bullion** – Often has lower premiums than competitors.

✓ **Provident Metals** – A solid choice for junk silver and collectible coins.

Local Coin Shops (If You Prefer In-Person Buying)

✓ Local coin shops offer **privacy**—no online transactions.

✓ You can inspect gold and silver **before buying**.

✓ Build a **relationship with a dealer** for future purchases.

Warning: Always check market prices before buying to avoid overpaying!

How to Store and Protect Your Gold and Silver

Owning physical metals means you need a **safe and secure place to store them**.

Best Storage Options:

✓ **Home Safe** – Best for quick access, but requires a high-quality safe (fireproof, waterproof, theft-resistant).

✓ **Private Vaults** – Secure storage outside the banking system (examples: Brinks, Loomis, or private depositories).

✓ **Safe Deposit Box (Bank)** – Offers security, but beware—banks could **lock down access in a financial crisis**.

Best Practice: Store metals in **multiple locations** to reduce risk.

How Much Gold and Silver Should You Own?

✓ **10-20% of your total net worth** in gold and silver is a common rule
.

✓ **More silver than gold** if you expect higher growth potential.

✓ **Some in physical form, some in ETFs/mining stocks** for liquidity.

Final Thoughts: Gold and Silver Are No Longer Optional—They Are Essential

Governments and central banks are **devaluing money faster than ever**, making gold and silver **the best protection against inflation and financial chaos**.

> ✓ **Physical metals provide financial security and long-term wealth preservation.**

> ✓ **ETFs and mining stocks offer additional investment opportunities.**

> ✓ **Choosing the right storage ensures your metals are safe.**

Now that you understand how to buy and store gold and silver, the next chapter will explore **the differences between physical and paper metals—why some investments may not be as safe as they seem.**

Chapter 9: Physical vs. Paper Metals – Understanding the Differences

Why Owning Gold and Silver in Your Hands is Safer Than Paper Investments

"If you don't hold it, you don't own it."

~ Precious Metals Investor Adage

When investing in gold and silver, you have two primary choices

✓ **Physical metals** (gold and silver coins, bars, bullion).

✓ **Paper metals** (ETFs, futures contracts, mining stocks).

While paper gold and silver may seem **easier and more convenient**, they come with **serious risks** that most investors **don't realize until it's too late**. History has shown that **governments, banks, and financial institutions manipulate paper metals markets**, making it difficult for investors to benefit from real price appreciation.

This chapter will break down the **key differences between physical and paper metals**, exposing the risks and benefits of each—so you can make an informed decision.

---

1. What Are Physical Metals?

Physical metals refer to **real, tangible gold and silver** that you can **hold in your hand**. When you own physical metals, there is **no counterparty risk**—you are not relying on a financial institution to give you access to your wealth.

Types of Physical Gold and Silver:

✓ **Coins** – Minted by governments and easy to trade. Examples:

- **Gold Coins**: American Gold Eagle, Canadian Maple Leaf, Krugerrand.

- **Silver Coins**: American Silver Eagle, Canadian Silver Maple Leaf, Austrian Philharmonic.

✓ **Bars** – Lower premiums than coins, best for large investments. Examples:

- **Gold Bars**: 1 oz, 10 oz, 1 kg, 400 oz bars.

- **Silver Bars**: 1 oz, 10 oz, 100 oz, 1,000 oz bars.

✓ **Junk Silver** – U.S. coins minted before **1965**, which contain **90% silver**. Cheap and widely recognized.

Benefits of Physical Metals:

✓ **No counterparty risk** – You own it outright, without depending on a bank or institution.

✓ **Can be used as real money** – Gold and silver have been used as currency for thousands of years
.
✓ **Portable wealth** – Unlike digital assets or bank accounts, metals are **private and secure**.

✓ **Cannot be hacked or frozen** – Bank accounts and ETFs can be **locked down in financial crises**.

Risks of Physical Metals:

✗ **Storage required** – You need a secure place to keep your metals.

✗ **Not instantly liquid** – Selling may take time, unlike stocks.

✗ **Higher premiums** – Coins and bars can cost more than the spot price.

Best For: Long-term investors who want to protect their wealth from inflation, financial crises, and bank failures.

2. What Are Paper Metals?

Paper metals refer to **gold and silver investments that exist only on paper**, without real metal backing them. These include **ETFs, futures contracts, and gold mining stocks**.

Types of Paper Gold and Silver:

✓ **Gold & Silver ETFs** – Exchange-traded funds that track the price of gold or silver.

- **Popular ETFs:** SPDR Gold Shares (GLD), iShares Silver Trust (SLV).

✓ **Futures Contracts** – Paper agreements to buy or sell gold/silver at a future date.

- Used by banks and traders, but often **not backed by real metal**.

✓ **Gold & Silver Mining Stocks** – Investing in companies that **mine gold and silver** rather than the metal itself.

- **Examples:** Barrick Gold (GOLD), Newmont (NEM), First Majestic Silver (AG).

Risks of Paper Metals:

✗ **You don't own real gold or silver** – Paper assets are just financial instruments that track prices.

✗ **Counterparty risk** – If the bank or institution fails, your investment could be **worthless**.

✗ **Can be frozen or restricted** – In a financial crisis, governments can **block access to ETFs and mining stocks**.

✗ **Gold ETFs may not have real metal backing** – Many ETFs issue **more paper gold than actual physical reserves**.

Best For: Short-term traders or those looking for liquidity, but NOT for true wealth protection.

3. The Biggest Risks of Paper Gold and Silver

A. ETFs and Futures May Not Have Real Metal

Many investors believe that gold ETFs like **GLD** or silver ETFs like **SLV** are backed by **physical gold and silver**. However, in reality, these funds often have **more paper claims than actual metal reserves**.

✓ A single ounce of gold may be "owned" by **dozens of investors** in the ETF system.

✓ ETFs don't allow investors to **redeem shares for actual gold or silver**—you are only holding a paper promise.

✓ In a crisis, ETF investors may **never get their metals**, as banks can refuse withdrawals.

If gold and silver ETFs were fully backed, why do central banks still buy real gold instead of ETFs?

B. Gold and Silver Markets Are Manipulated

The **paper gold and silver markets** are highly manipulated by major banks and financial institutions. They use **naked short selling**, which allows them to **sell gold and silver they don't actually own**, suppressing prices.

> ✓ In 2020, JPMorgan Chase was **fined $920 million** for manipulating gold and silver markets.

> ✓ The paper metals market trades **hundreds of times more gold and silver than physically exists**.

> ✓ If banks are manipulating prices, how can paper metal investors trust the system?

C. Governments Can Confiscate Paper Metals – But Not Physical Gold and Silver

History shows that **paper assets can be frozen, seized, or taxed heavily** in a crisis.

> ✓ **1933 – U.S. Gold Confiscation:** President Franklin D. Roosevelt issued **Executive Order 6102**, forcing Americans to turn in their gold.

> ✓ **Bank Bail-Ins (Cyprus 2013 & Canada 2023) –** Governments froze bank accounts and took depositor money during financial crises.

> ✓ **If your gold and silver are stored in a bank or ETF, they can be confiscated or frozen.**

Physical gold and silver stored outside the banking system offer true financial security.

---

4. What's the Best Investment: Physical or Paper Metals?

Physical Gold & Silver – Best for Wealth Protection

✓ No counterparty risk

✓ Cannot be printed, hacked, or frozen

✓ Holds value in a crisis

Gold & Silver ETFs – Best for Liquidity

✓ Easy to buy and sell quickly

✓ No need for storage

✓ Good for short-term price speculation

Gold & Silver Mining Stocks – Best for High-Risk, High-Reward Investing

✓ Potential for bigger gains if metals rise

✓ Companies may pay dividends

✓ Stocks can go bankrupt, unlike real gold

5. How to Protect Yourself: The Best Strategy

The best approach is to **combine physical metals with strategic paper investments** to balance **security and liquidity**.

> ✓ Hold at least 50-80% of your precious metals in physical form.

> ✓ Use ETFs for short-term price speculation, but never rely on them as your primary holding.

> ✓ Consider mining stocks as a high-risk, high-reward opportunity, but not as a replacement for real gold and silver.

Conclusion: If You Don't Hold It, You Don't Own It

Paper gold and silver can be useful for trading, but **they are not a substitute for real metal ownership**. If the financial system collapses, **only physical gold and silver will protect your wealth**.

> ✓ ETFs and futures contracts may disappear overnight in a crisis.

> ✓ Gold and silver in your possession cannot be seized, frozen, or manipulated.

> ✓ Those who hold real metals will always have an advantage over those relying on paper promises.

In the next chapter, we will discuss **government confiscation and capital controls—how governments have targeted gold and silver investors in the past, and how to protect yourself in the future.**

Chapter 10: Government Confiscation and Capital Controls – Could It Happen Again?

How Governments Have Targeted Gold and Silver Investors in the Past—And How to Protect Yourself Today

"The few who understand the system will either be so interested in its profits or so dependent upon its favors, that there will be no opposition from that class... The great body of the people, mentally incapable of comprehending, will bear its burden without complaint."

— Rothschild Banking Family

For centuries, governments have manipulated money, **debased currencies, and imposed financial controls** to maintain power. When economic crises hit, they often **target gold and silver owners**—the very people who are trying to protect their wealth.

Throughout history, **gold confiscation, wealth taxes, and capital controls** have been used to prevent citizens from escaping financial repression. Today, as global debt skyrockets and economic uncertainty grows, it is crucial to **understand these risks and prepare accordingly**.

In this chapter, we will explore:

✓ **How governments have seized gold and restricted capital flows in the past.**

✓ **Why gold and silver investors could be targeted again.**

✓ **How to protect your wealth from confiscation and financial repression.**

1. Historical Gold Confiscation: The 1933 U.S. Executive Order

One of the most infamous examples of gold confiscation occurred in the **United States in 1933**. During the Great Depression, President **Franklin D. Roosevelt issued Executive Order 6102**, requiring all citizens to **turn in their gold to the government**.

What Happened?

✓ The government **outlawed private gold ownership** and forced citizens to exchange their gold for **$20.67 per ounce**.

✓ Shortly after, the government **devalued the dollar by 40%**, raising the official price of gold to **$35 per ounce**.

✓ Americans **who complied lost wealth overnight**—while the government profited.

Lessons from 1933:

✓ Governments **can and will confiscate assets** when it benefits them.

✓ Gold owners who **held onto their metal illegally** preserved their wealth.

✓ **If gold is stored in banks or safety deposit boxes, it is vulnerable to seizure.**

Key Takeaway: If governments face economic collapse, they may turn to **gold confiscation again**.

2. More Recent Examples of Capital Controls and Financial Repression

Confiscation isn't the only risk—**capital controls, bank bail-ins, and wealth taxes** are modern ways governments restrict financial freedom.

A. Cyprus Bank Bail-In (2013) – Depositor Money Seized

During the 2013 banking crisis in **Cyprus**, the government froze bank accounts and seized **up to 47.5% of deposits** over €100,000 to bail out failing banks.

> ✓ **Citizens had no warning**—bank accounts were frozen overnight.

> ✓ **People rushed to withdraw cash and buy gold**—but it was too late.

> ✓ **Those who held gold and silver outside the banking system were protected.**

B. India's Gold Crackdown (2016-2017)

The Indian government **restricted gold imports and penalized cash transactions** to prevent citizens from moving wealth into **physical gold**.

> ✓ **Gold imports were heavily taxed** to discourage private ownership.

> ✓ **Banks were pressured to report gold purchases** to the government.

> ✓ **Digital payments were promoted over cash and gold transactions.**

Lesson: When governments struggle with debt, they try to limit gold ownership and push people into **digital banking and fiat money.**

C. Venezuela's Gold Confiscation and Hyperinflation (2010s-Present)

Venezuela's economic collapse led to **gold confiscation and government crackdowns on wealth.**

✓ **The government nationalized gold mines**, preventing private ownership.

✓ **Citizens were banned from holding gold bullion** without government approval.

✓ **Hyperinflation forced people to trade in gold dust—** paper money became worthless.

Key Takeaway: When fiat money collapses, governments turn to **gold confiscation and currency controls** to survive.

---

3. How Governments Could Target Gold and Silver Investors Again

Governments are facing **massive debt burdens**, rising inflation, and financial instability. If they **run out of options**, they may try to **confiscate wealth** using these methods:

✓ **Gold Nationalization** – Requiring citizens to sell gold to the government at **artificially low prices** (like in 1933).

✓ **Wealth Taxes** – A direct tax on **gold holdings, cash savings, and investments**.

✓ **Banning Cash Transactions** – Forcing people into **digital banking**, where their money is **fully controlled**.

✓ **Digital Currency Control (CBDCs)** – Governments could replace cash with **Central Bank Digital Currencies (CBDCs)**, allowing **total financial surveillance** and **preventing escape into gold and silver**.

If a financial crisis occurs, gold and silver investors will likely be among the first targeted.

4. How to Protect Your Wealth from Confiscation and Capital Controls

While governments have **confiscated wealth in the past**, there are **ways to reduce your risk** and protect your gold and silver holdings.

A. Store Gold and Silver Privately, Outside the Banking System

✓ **Do not store gold in a bank safety deposit box**—it can be **seized or locked down in a crisis**.

✓ **Use a home safe**—high-quality, fireproof, theft-resistant safes provide protection.

✓ **Consider private vaults**—secure storage facilities outside of the banking system.

B. Diversify Holdings Across Different Locations

✓ Keep **some metals at home** for easy access in an emergency.

✓ Store **larger amounts in private vaults** or offshore locations.

✓ **Split holdings between multiple locations** to reduce risk of full confiscation.

C. Own Gold and Silver in Multiple Forms

✓ **Bullion coins and bars** – Highly liquid and easy to trade.

✓ **Junk silver (pre-1965 coins)** – Less likely to be confiscated due to small denominations.

✓ **Gold and silver jewelry** – Not typically targeted by governments.

D. Consider International Storage and Offshore Vaults

For larger gold and silver holdings, **offshore storage in politically stable countries** may provide protection.

> ✓ **Switzerland, Singapore, and Liechtenstein** have strong private vault systems.

> ✓ Private vaults like **Brink's, Loomis, and Goldmoney** offer secure storage outside government reach.

> ✓ **Storing some metals abroad** adds an extra layer of financial security.

Key Takeaway: Having all your gold and silver in one place is a risk. Diversify storage locations to reduce the chances of government seizure.

E. Avoid Digital and Traceable Transactions When Buying Gold and Silver

Governments can track digital transactions and **monitor who is buying gold and silver**. To protect privacy:

> ✓ Buy some metals **with cash from local coin shops** (within legal limits).

> ✓ Avoid excessive **bank transfers for bullion purchases**.

> ✓ Consider **peer-to-peer transactions** when selling metals to avoid tracking.

The less information the government has about your holdings, the safer you are.

Final Thoughts: Financial Freedom Starts with Gold and Silver Ownership

History proves that governments will always **prioritize their survival over individual financial freedom**. When a financial crisis strikes, they will use **capital controls, bank bail-ins, and even gold confiscation** to protect their system.

> ✓ If **gold and silver were useless**, why do governments try so hard to **limit private ownership**?

> ✓ If fiat money were stable, why are **central banks buying gold** while telling citizens not to?

The truth is clear:

Gold and silver are the ultimate forms of financial independence.

In the next chapter, we will discuss **how to store your wealth securely—choosing the best storage options for gold and silver to keep your investments safe from theft, government seizure, and financial crises.**

Chapter 11: Storing Your Wealth – Best Practices for Gold and Silver Storage

How to Keep Your Precious Metals Safe from Theft, Confiscation, and Financial Crises

"The more you diversify your paper wealth into real wealth—gold, silver, and tangible assets—the safer you will be."

~ Ron Paul

Investing in gold and silver is **only half the battle**—the other half is ensuring that **your metals are stored securely and protected from theft, government confiscation, and financial collapse**.

Precious metals are unique because they:

✓ Have **no counterparty risk** (unlike bank deposits or digital investments).

✓ **Store value privately** without reliance on the banking system.

✓ Are **highly portable** and can be hidden or stored in multiple locations.

However, this also means that **gold and silver require careful storage planning**. If your metals are stolen, confiscated, or lost, **there's no "reset button" to get them back**.

This chapter will cover

:✓ **The best storage options for gold and silver.**

✓ **How to balance security and accessibility.**

✓ **The risks of storing metals in banks.**

✓ **Why offshore vaults may be a good option.**

1. Choosing the Right Storage Strategy

There is no **one-size-fits-all** solution for storing gold and silver. The best storage method depends on:

✓ **How much metal you own.**

✓ **How frequently you plan to access it.**

✓ **The level of security and privacy you need.**

Most investors use a **combination of different storage methods** to spread risk and ensure they have **easy access when needed**.

2. Storing Gold and Silver at Home

Keeping precious metals **at home** offers **immediate access** in case of economic crises, banking restrictions, or personal financial emergencies.

Best Practices for Home Storage:

✓ **Use a high-quality safe** – Fireproof, waterproof, and heavy enough to prevent easy removal.

✓ **Diversify hiding spots** – Avoid keeping all metals in one place.

✓ **Use decoy valuables** – Have fake valuables to distract burglars.

✓ **Keep a portion in easily accessible locations** – In case of emergencies.

The Best Types of Safes for Home Storage:

✓ **Fireproof and waterproof safes** – Protect against natural disasters.

✓ **Hidden safes** – Safes disguised as furniture, air vents, or false walls.

✓ **Heavy-duty floor safes** – Anchored into concrete, difficult to remove.

Pro Tip: Store small amounts in different locations rather than keeping all metals in one place.

Risks of Home Storage:

✗ **Theft risk** – If someone knows you own gold and silver, you could be targeted.

✗ **Fire or natural disasters** – If your house burns down, metals could be lost.

✗ **No insurance coverage** – Many home insurance policies **do not cover** precious metals.

3. Storing Gold and Silver in a Private Vault (Non-Bank Storage)

For larger gold and silver holdings, **private vaults and depositories** offer professional security **outside the banking system**.

Best Private Vault Options:

✓ **Brink's Global Services** – Trusted worldwide security and vault services.

✓ **Loomis International** – Secure vault storage for large investors.

✓ **Goldmoney** – Provides allocated and insured gold storage in multiple countries.

✓ **The Royal Mint (UK)** – Offers government-backed vault storage for gold.

Benefits of Private Vaults:

✓ **Highly secure** – 24/7 surveillance and insurance coverage.

✓ **Outside the banking system** – Safe from financial collapses and bank bail-ins.

✓ **Can store large amounts** – Suitable for high-net-worth investors.

Risks of Private Vaults:

✗ **Limited immediate access** – Not as convenient as home storage.

✗ **Storage fees** – Monthly or annual charges apply.

✗ **Government regulations** – Some countries could impose gold restrictions.

Pro Tip: Choose vaults in **politically stable countries** with strong private property laws.

4. The Risks of Storing Gold and Silver in Banks

Many new investors assume that **bank safety deposit boxes** are a secure way to store gold and silver. However, this comes with **serious risks**.

Why Banks Are a Bad Place for Precious Metals:

✗ **Banks can freeze access** – During financial crises, governments have restricted bank withdrawals and deposit box access.

✗ **No insurance on metals** – Bank safety deposit boxes are **not insured** by the bank or FDIC.

✗ **Government confiscation risk** – In 1933, U.S. citizens who stored gold in banks had it confiscated.

✗ **Bank closures and bail-ins** – In Cyprus (2013), banks **seized deposits** to cover debt.

Key Takeaway: If your gold and silver are in a bank, they **belong to the bank—not you.**

5. Offshore Storage – Diversifying Wealth Internationally

For investors with significant gold and silver holdings, **offshore vault storage** provides an extra layer of protection **from local government overreach**.

Best Countries for Offshore Gold Storage:

✓ **Switzerland** – Strong banking privacy laws and private vaults

.

✓ **Singapore** – One of the safest countries with secure gold storage.

✓ **Liechtenstein** – Known for **low taxation and strong asset protection laws**.

✓ **New Zealand** – A stable and gold-friendly nation.

Benefits of Offshore Gold Storage:

✓ **Diversifies risk away from a single government's control.**

✓ **Protected from bank bail-ins and capital controls.**

✓ **Held in private vaults, outside the banking system.**

Risks of Offshore Gold Storage:

✗ **Less accessibility** – You may need to travel to retrieve metals.

✗ **Government restrictions on moving money or gold abroad.**

✗ **Dependence on political stability in the storage country.**

Pro Tip: Consider spreading gold and silver across **multiple jurisdictions** for added protection.

6. Gold and Silver Insurance – Should You Get It?

For investors holding **large amounts of physical metals**, getting **insurance coverage** can help protect against theft, loss, or natural disasters.

Best Ways to Insure Precious Metals:

✓ **Private insurance companies** – Some offer specialized bullion coverage.

✓ **Storage vaults with built-in insurance** – Many private vaults automatically insure holdings.

✓ **Lloyd's of London** – A leading provider of precious metals insurance.

When Insurance is Worth It:

✓ If you hold over **$50,000 worth of gold and silver**.

✓ If you **store metals at home or in a private vault**.

✓ If you live in an area with **high burglary risks or natural disasters**.

Key Takeaway: If you have **significant holdings**, insurance is a smart option.

7. Storing Silver vs. Gold – Different Storage Needs

✓ **Gold is more compact** – A **$100,000 investment in gold** weighs only **5 pounds**, making it easy to store.

✓ **Silver takes up more space** – The same investment in silver weighs **over 300 pounds**.

✓ **Silver tarnishes over time** – Store in airtight containers or Mylar bags.

✓ **Silver is more practical for transactions** – Small silver coins may be easier to use in a crisis.

Best Practice: Store gold for long-term wealth protection and **silver for everyday transactions in an economic crisis**.

Conclusion: Store Smart, Stay Secure

Proper storage is **just as important as buying gold and silver**. A smart strategy involves:

✓ **Keeping some metals at home for emergencies.**

✓ **Using private vaults for larger holdings.**

✓ **Avoiding bank storage due to confiscation risks.**

✓ **Considering offshore vaults for international diversification.**

Gold and Silver Are Financial Insurance—But Only If They're Stored Safely.

In the next chapter, we'll discuss **the future of money—can gold and silver regain their throne in an age of digital currencies and financial uncertainty?**

Chapter 12: Taking Action to Protect Your Wealth

A Step-by-Step Guide to Securing Your Financial Future with Gold and Silver

"The time to repair the roof is when the sun is shining."

~ John F. Kennedy

Throughout this book, we've explored the **history, necessity, and power of gold and silver** as real money. We've seen how governments **devalue currencies, manipulate markets, and restrict financial freedom**—all while quietly stockpiling gold themselves.

Now it's time to take action. The smartest investors don't wait for a crisis to hit before protecting their wealth—they prepare in advance.

This chapter provides a **step-by-step plan to secure your financial future with precious metals**, including:

✓ How much gold and silver you should own.

✓ Where and how to buy safely.

✓ Storage strategies to keep your metals secure.

✓ How to use gold and silver in a financial crisis.

If you're serious about preserving your wealth, the time to act is **now**.

Step 1: Determine How Much Gold and Silver You Need

There's no **one-size-fits-all** amount of gold and silver to own—it depends on your financial goals.

A. Gold and Silver as a Percentage of Your Portfolio

> ✓ **10-20% of total net worth** – Recommended for most investors as a hedge against inflation.

> ✓ **30-50% or more** – For those who expect severe financial crises or hyperinflation.

> ✓ **5-10% in silver, 10-15% in gold** – A balanced mix that provides both liquidity and long-term stability.

If you hold too little, you may not be protected. If you hold too much, you may lack liquidity for daily expenses.

B. Gold vs. Silver – Which Should You Buy?

> ✓ **Gold** is a store of wealth, best for **long-term savings and preserving purchasing power**.

> ✓ **Silver** is more affordable and practical for **smaller transactions and daily use in a crisis**.

Factor	Gold	Silver
Best for	Wealth preservation	Inflation hedge, barter
Storage	Compact, easy to store	Takes up more space
Price Volatility	Lower	Higher
Industrial Demand	Limited	High (electronics, solar, etc.)
Government Confiscation Risk	Higher	Lower

✓ **If you want stability, buy more gold.**

✓ **If you want liquidity and future spending potential, buy more silver.**

Step 2: Where and How to Buy Gold and Silver Safely

Not all gold and silver sellers are reputable. Scams and overpriced products are common.

A. Best Places to Buy Gold and Silver

✓ **Trusted Online Dealers:**

- **APMEX** (American Precious Metals Exchange)
- **JM Bullion**
- **SD Bullion**
- **Provident Metals**

✓ Local Coin Shops:

- Offers **cash transactions for privacy**.
- Can inspect the metal **before purchasing**.
- Best for **small silver and gold coin purchases**.

✓ Direct from Mints:

- **U.S. Mint, Royal Canadian Mint, Perth Mint.**
- Official, guaranteed purity but sometimes **higher premiums**.

B. What Type of Gold and Silver to Buy?

✓ Gold Coins: American Gold Eagles, Canadian Maple Leafs, Krugerrands.

✓ Silver Coins: American Silver Eagles, Canadian Silver Maple Leafs.

✓ Gold Bars: 1 oz, 10 oz, 1 kg, or 400 oz bars
.

✓ Silver Bars: 10 oz, 100 oz, or 1,000 oz bars
.

✓ Junk Silver: U.S. dimes, quarters, and half dollars **minted before 1965** (90% silver).

C. Avoiding Scams and Overpriced Metals

✗ **Avoid "rare" or collectible coins** – Dealers mark them up significantly.

✗ **Avoid eBay, Craigslist, or unknown sellers** – Many counterfeits exist.

✗ **Check the current spot price** – Don't pay **excessive premiums** over the metal's actual value.

✓ **Best strategy:** Stick to **well-known bullion coins and bars from reputable dealers**.

Step 3: Storing Your Gold and Silver Securely

Storage is critical—your investment is only safe if it's **protected from theft, loss, or confiscation**.

A. Home Storage (Best for Immediate Access)

✓ **Use a high-quality safe** – Fireproof, waterproof, and anchored securely.

✓ **Split holdings into multiple locations** – Don't keep everything in one place.

✓ **Consider hiding some metals in creative places** – Decoy safes, hidden compartments, etc.

Avoid storing metals in bank safety deposit boxes – Governments can seize them in financial crises!

B. Private Vault Storage (Best for Large Holdings)

For larger investments, **private, non-bank vaults** offer professional security.

✓ **Recommended Vaults:**

- **Brink's Global Services**
- **Loomis International**
- **Goldmoney**
- **The Royal Mint (UK)**

✓ **Benefits of Private Vaults:**

- Safe from **theft and government bank bail-ins**.
- **Fully insured** storage options.
- No risk of losing access due to financial restrictions.

Avoid bank-controlled vaults—they can be frozen or seized!

Step 4: Using Gold and Silver in a Financial Crisis

If fiat money collapses, how will you use gold and silver?

A. Gold for Large Purchases, Silver for Everyday Transactions

✓ **Gold bars and coins** – Best for **storing long-term wealth**.

✓ **Silver coins and junk silver** – Best for **bartering and small transactions**.

B. Where Can You Use Precious Metals in a Crisis?

✓ **Local barter networks** – Silver and gold will be accepted for goods/services.

✓ **Private trade with farmers, mechanics, doctors, and small businesses**

.

✓ **International markets** – Gold will always be exchangeable for stable currencies.

Pro Tip: Hold **small silver coins** for daily transactions—gold is too valuable for everyday purchases.

Step 5: Staying Ahead of Government Restrictions

Governments **may try to restrict gold and silver ownership** through taxes, regulations, or even confiscation. Protect yourself by:

✓ **Keeping some metals anonymous** – Buy with cash when possible.

✓ **Storing some holdings in offshore vaults** – Countries like Switzerland and Singapore offer strong protections.

✓ **Diversifying your wealth** – Don't rely entirely on gold; include land, food, and essential assets.

If governments didn't see gold as a threat to fiat currency, they wouldn't discourage private ownership.

Final Thoughts: Act Now Before It's Too Late

✓ **Gold and silver have survived every financial collapse in history**

.

✓ **Fiat money always loses value—precious metals retain purchasing power.**

✓ **The best time to protect your wealth is BEFORE a crisis hits.**

Your Next Steps:

✓ **Decide how much gold and silver to buy (10-20% of your portfolio recommended).**

✓ **Buy from reputable sources (APMEX, JM Bullion, local coin shops).**

✓ **Store metals securely (home safe, private vaults, avoid banks).**

✓ **Stay informed—watch economic trends and be prepared for financial instability.**

Final Words: Wealth is Preserved by Those Who Prepare

The financial system is changing, and the risks of inflation, digital currency control, and economic collapse are growing. Gold and silver are **not just investments—they are insurance for your financial future**.

The greatest wealth transfer in history is happening now. Will you be on the right side of it?

Take action today. Secure your gold and silver. **Protect your wealth before it's too late.**

Epilogue: The End of One Era, the Beginning of Another

The global financial system is at a crossroads. Decades of reckless monetary policy, runaway debt, and government overreach have created a fragile economy that is increasingly unstable and unsustainable. The warning signs are everywhere—rising inflation, devalued currencies, economic crises, and increasing government intervention in financial markets.

Throughout history, when fiat currencies have failed, when governments have overextended themselves, and when trust in financial institutions has crumbled, one thing has always remained constant: gold and silver endure.

This book has shown why gold and silver are more than just commodities. They are true money, timeless stores of value, and financial insurance against the collapse of paper currencies. The lessons of history are clear: those who rely solely on government-backed money risk losing their wealth, while those who understand the power of real, tangible assets like gold and silver position themselves for financial security.

A New Financial Era is Unfolding

We are witnessing a shift in the global economic order. Countries like China and Russia are accumulating gold at record levels, international trade is moving away from the U.S. dollar, and central banks are exploring alternative monetary systems. The trust in fiat currencies is weakening, and people around the world are rediscovering the importance of sound money

.At the same time, technological advancements are reshaping the way gold and silver can be used as money. Gold-backed cryptocurrencies, decentralized financial systems, and blockchain technology are laying the groundwork for a new financial paradigm—one that could return gold and silver to their rightful place at the center of global commerce.

The question is no longer **if** the financial system will change, but when and how.

Your Financial Future is in Your Hands

No one can predict the future with certainty, but history offers valuable guidance. Those who take control of their financial future today—by owning real assets, diversifying their holdings, and preparing for economic shifts—will be far better positioned than those who remain dependent on the failing fiat system.

> ✓ If you've read this book and haven't yet taken action, now is the time.
> ✓ If you've already begun accumulating gold and silver, continue strengthening your position.
>
> ✓ If you understand the risks of the current system, educate others and help them protect their wealth, too.

The financial system of the future will look very different from what we know today. Gold and silver will remain constant, as they always have. The choice is yours: will you prepare for the coming changes, or will you wait until it's too late?

By securing your wealth in gold and silver, you are not only protecting your financial future—you are embracing a monetary system that has stood the test of time.

A new era is coming. Make sure you are ready.

Bibliography

This book draws on historical events, economic principles, and financial data from a variety of sources, including books, research papers, government reports, and expert analyses on gold, silver, monetary policy, and financial crises. Below is a list of key references that have informed the discussion on precious metals, inflation, fiat currency, and economic history.

Books & Publications

- Bernanke, Ben S. *The Courage to Act: A Memoir of a Crisis and Its Aftermath.* W.W. Norton & Company, 2015.

- Dalio, Ray. *The Changing World Order: Why Nations Succeed and Fail.* Avid Reader Press, 2021.

- Ferguson, Niall. *The Ascent of Money: A Financial History of the World.* Penguin Books, 2008.

- Gilder, George. *The Scandal of Money: Why Wall Street Recovers but the Economy Never Does.* Regnery Publishing, 2016.

- Greenspan, Alan. *The Age of Turbulence: Adventures in a New World.* Penguin Books, 2007.

- Griffin, G. Edward. *The Creature from Jekyll Island: A Second Look at the Federal Reserve.* American Media, 1994.

- Hayek, Friedrich A. *The Denationalization of Money.* Institute of Economic Affairs, 1976.

- Mishkin, Frederic S. *The Economics of Money, Banking, and Financial Markets.* Pearson, 2018.

- Paul, Ron. *The Case for Gold: A Minority Report of the U.S. Gold Commission.* Ludwig von Mises Institute, 1982.

- Rickards, James. *The Death of Money: The Coming Collapse of the International Monetary System.* Portfolio, 2014.

- Rothbard, Murray N. *What Has Government Done to Our Money?* Ludwig von Mises Institute, 1963.

- Rothbard, Murray N. *The Case for a 100% Gold Dollar.* Ludwig von Mises Institute, 2001.

- Saifedean Ammous. *The Bitcoin Standard: The Decentralized Alternative to Central Banking.* Wiley, 2018.

- Skidelsky, Robert. *Keynes: The Return of the Master.* Penguin Books, 2009.

- Taleb, Nassim Nicholas. *The Black Swan: The Impact of the Highly Improbable.* Random House, 2007.

- Turk, James, and John Rubino. *The Collapse of the Dollar and How to Profit from It: Make a Fortune by Investing in Gold and Other Hard Assets.* Doubleday, 2004.

Articles & Reports

- Bank for International Settlements (BIS). *Annual Economic Report 2022.*

- Federal Reserve Bank of St. Louis. *The History of U.S. Inflation and Money Supply Growth.*

- International Monetary Fund (IMF). *The Global Debt Crisis: Current Trends and Future Risks.*

- Kitco News. *Gold Price Forecasts: Historical Trends and Market Analysis.*

- Mises Institute. *Fiat Money and Its Consequences on the Economy.*

- World Gold Council. *Gold Demand Trends Report, 2023.*
- World Silver Institute. *Annual Silver Market Review, 2023.*

Historical Documents & Government Records

- Executive Order 6102, *Requiring Gold Coin, Gold Bullion and Gold Certificates to be Delivered to the Government*, Signed by President Franklin D. Roosevelt, April 5, 1933.

- Nixon, Richard M. *Address to the Nation on Domestic Economic Policies*, August 15, 1971.

- U.S. Department of the Treasury. *The Bretton Woods Agreement and the Transition to Fiat Currency (1944-1971).*

- Weimar Republic Central Bank Records, *Hyperinflation in Germany (1919-1923).*

Websites & Online Resources

- **BullionStar** – Research on gold and silver market trends.

- **CoinWeek** – Analysis of historical and modern bullion markets.

- **GoldMoney.com** – Reports on central bank gold holdings and gold-backed digital currencies.

- **ShadowStats.com** – Analysis of real inflation rates and economic statistics.

- **ZeroHedge.com** – Independent financial analysis and monetary policy critique.

Acknowledgment of AI-Assisted Research

The research, organization, and editing of this book were supplemented by AI-powered tools to enhance clarity, formatting, and accuracy. However, the core ideas, historical references, and financial principles are based on well-documented sources, economic history, and the real-world performance of gold and silver over time.

This bibliography provides a foundation for further exploration into the history, economics, and investment strategies of gold and silver. Readers who wish to deepen their understanding of monetary policy, inflation, and financial crises are encouraged to explore these works and continue their research into sound money and wealth preservation strategies.

Glossary

This glossary provides definitions of key terms related to gold, silver, monetary policy, and financial markets that are discussed throughout this book. Understanding these terms will help readers navigate the complexities of the global economy and the role of precious metals in wealth preservation.

A

Asset Bubble – A situation in which the price of an asset (e.g., stocks, real estate, or gold) rises significantly above its intrinsic value due to speculation and excessive demand.

Austrian Economics – A school of economic thought that emphasizes free markets, sound money (such as gold and silver), and limited government intervention in the economy.

B

Bank Run – A financial crisis in which a large number of depositors withdraw their money from a bank due to fears of insolvency, often leading to the bank's collapse.

Bimetallism – A monetary system in which both gold and silver are used as legal tender, typically with a fixed exchange ratio between the two metals.

Bretton Woods Agreement (1944) – The international agreement that established the U.S. dollar as the world's reserve currency, pegged to gold at $35 per ounce, and fixed exchange rates for other major currencies. The system collapsed in 1971 when the U.S. abandoned the gold standard.

Bullion – Physical gold or silver in the form of bars, coins, or rounds, valued primarily by metal content rather than collectible or numismatic value.

C

Capital Controls – Government-imposed restrictions on the flow of money, assets, or precious metals in and out of a country, often used during financial crises.

Central Bank – A government-controlled financial institution that manages a country's money supply, controls interest rates, and oversees commercial banks (e.g., Federal Reserve, European Central Bank).

Central Bank Digital Currency (CBDC) – A government-backed digital currency that could replace traditional cash and allow central banks greater control over financial transactions.

Coinage Act of 1792 – The U.S. law that established gold and silver as the basis of the nation's monetary system, creating the U.S. dollar with a fixed ratio of silver to gold.

Confiscation (Gold Confiscation) – A government act of forcibly seizing private gold holdings, as occurred in the U.S. under Executive Order 6102 in 1933.

Counterparty Risk – The risk that a financial institution, government, or other party will default on its obligations, making physical gold and silver preferable to paper-based financial assets.

D

Debt Crisis – A situation where governments, businesses, or individuals accumulate unsustainable levels of debt, leading to economic instability or financial collapse.

Debasement – The practice of reducing the metal content of coins while maintaining their face value, effectively inflating the currency (e.g., the Roman Empire's devaluation of the silver denarius).

Deflation – A decrease in the general price level of goods and services, often caused by reduced money supply or economic contraction.

Dollarization – The process by which a foreign country adopts the U.S. dollar as its official currency due to instability in its own monetary system.

E

Executive Order 6102 (1933) – The U.S. government mandate issued by President Franklin D. Roosevelt, making it illegal for American citizens to own most forms of gold and requiring them to surrender their gold to the government in exchange for paper dollars.

Exchange-Traded Fund (ETF) – A financial product that tracks the price of an asset, such as gold or silver, but often lacks direct backing by physical metals (e.g., SPDR Gold Shares - GLD, iShares Silver Trust - SLV).

F

Fiat Currency – Government-issued money not backed by a physical commodity like gold or silver. Its value is based solely on public trust and government decree.

Fractional Reserve Banking – A banking system where banks are only required to hold a fraction of their deposits in reserve, allowing them to create money by lending out more than they actually hold.

Futures Contract – A financial agreement to buy or sell an asset (such as gold or silver) at a set price on a future date. These contracts are often used for speculation and price manipulation in the metals markets.

G

Gold Standard – A monetary system in which a country's currency is directly linked to a fixed amount of gold, preventing governments from printing money without having the gold to back it.

Gold-to-Silver Ratio – A measure of how many ounces of silver are needed to purchase one ounce of gold. Historically, the ratio has ranged from 15:1 to over 80:1, with a higher ratio indicating that silver is undervalued relative to gold.

Gresham's Law – The economic principle stating that "bad money drives out good money"—when governments debase currency, people hoard gold and silver and spend the devalued money instead.

H

Hard Assets – Tangible assets such as gold, silver, real estate, and commodities, which retain intrinsic value regardless of government policies or inflation.

Hyperinflation – An extreme and rapid increase in prices, often exceeding 50% per month, rendering a currency worthless (e.g., Weimar Germany in the 1920s, Zimbabwe in the 2000s, Venezuela in recent years).

I

Inflation – The decline of a currency's purchasing power, leading to rising prices of goods and services due to an increase in money supply.

Intrinsic Value – The inherent worth of an asset, independent of government policy. Gold and silver have intrinsic value because they cannot be created or devalued by central banks.

M

Monetary Debasement – The deliberate destruction of a currency's value through excessive money printing, reducing purchasing power over time.

Monetary Policy – Actions taken by central banks to control money supply, interest rates, and inflation, often leading to economic distortions.

P

Precious Metals – Naturally occurring metals like gold, silver, platinum, and palladium, valued for their scarcity, durability, and use as money.

Purchasing Power – The amount of goods and services that money can buy. Gold and silver preserve purchasing power, while fiat currencies lose purchasing power over time due to inflation.

S

Safe Haven Asset – An asset that retains or increases in value during economic uncertainty, such as gold and silver.

Silver Standard – A monetary system where currency is backed by silver instead of gold. The U.S. operated under a bimetallic system (gold and silver) until 1873.

Spot Price – The current market price of gold or silver for immediate delivery, as opposed to futures contracts that set a price for future settlement.

W

Weimar Hyperinflation (1921-1923) – The economic collapse in post-World War I Germany, where excessive money printing caused the German mark to become worthless, forcing people to use gold, silver, and foreign currencies for trade.

Conclusion

Understanding these financial and economic terms is crucial for protecting your wealth in an era of monetary uncertainty. Gold and silver have been trusted forms of money for thousands of years, and as history has shown, those who understand sound money principles are best prepared for financial instability.

By owning physical gold and silver, staying informed, and applying the knowledge in this book, you can take control of your financial future and ensure that your wealth remains protected—no matter what happens to fiat currencies.